Welcome to

THE TENNIS PLAYER'S EXCUSE HANDBOOK

Lunar Press is an independent publishing company that cares greatly about the accuracy of its content.

If you notice any inaccuracies or have anything that you would like to discuss, then please email us at
lunarpresspublishers@gmail.com.

Enjoy!

© Copyright 2024 - All rights reserved.

The content contained within this book may not be reproduced, duplicated or transmitted without direct written permission from the author or the publisher.

Under no circumstances will any blame or legal responsibility be held against the publisher, or author, for any damages, reparation, or monetary loss due to the information contained within this book, either directly or indirectly.

Legal Notice:

This book is copyright protected. It is only for personal use. You cannot amend, distribute, sell, use, quote or paraphrase any part, or the content within this book, without the consent of the author or publisher.

Disclaimer Notice:

Please note the information contained within this document is for educational and entertainment purposes only. All effort has been executed to present accurate, up to date, reliable, complete information. No warranties of any kind are declared or implied. Readers acknowledge that the author is not engaged in the rendering of legal, financial, medical or professional advice. The content within this book has been derived from various sources. Please consult a licensed professional before attempting any techniques outlined in this book.

By reading this document, the reader agrees that under no circumstances is the author responsible for any losses, direct or indirect, that are incurred as a result of the use of the information contained within this document, including, but not limited to, errors, omissions, or inaccuracies.

IF YOU ENJOY THIS BOOK, CHECK OUT...

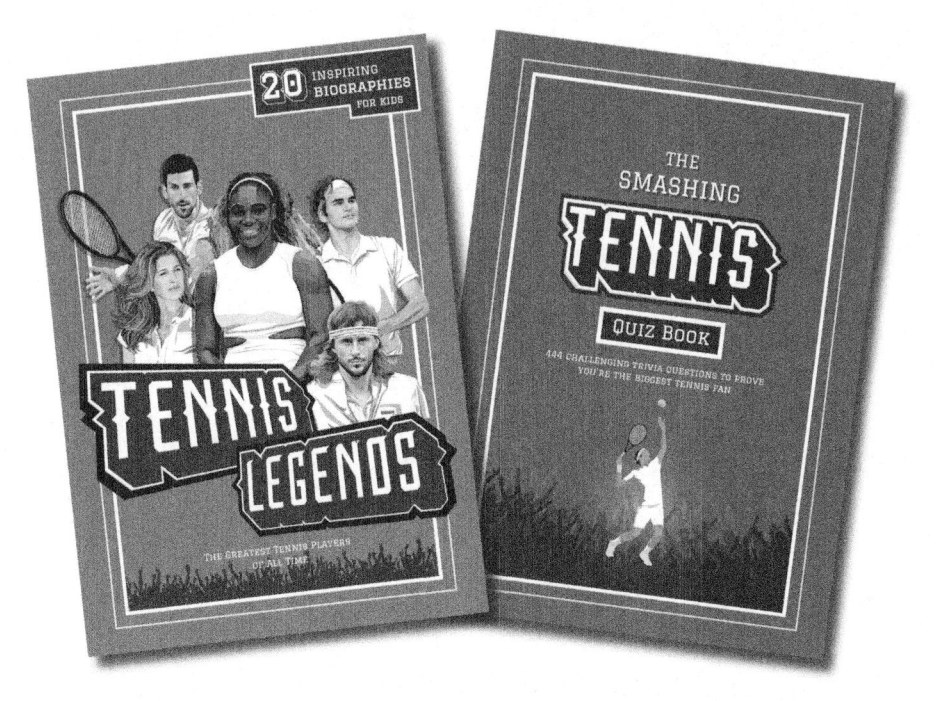

COMPLETE THE SET!

Tennis Legends is a collection of 20 illustrated biographies of the best players to ever step onto the court and is a great way for young tennis fans to learn about the legends of the past.

The Smashing Tennis Quiz is a collection of 444 challenging trivia questions - test yourself or compete with a family quiz night!

CONTENTS

Game, Set, Excuse: 7
The Greatest Excuses in Professional Tennis History

I Wasn't Ready: 26
The Best Personal Excuses

It's Not My Fault: 44
Marvellous Opponent-Based Excuses

Blame The Elements: 65
Excuses About the Conditions

New Balls Please: 71
Everyday Equipment Excuses in Tennis

You Cannot Be Serious: 81
Timeless Tennis Complaints

Courtside Clichés: 88
Classic Tennis Stereotypes

WARM UP

The origins of tennis date back to France in the 12th century, which means humanity has had nearly 900 years to perfect the art of excuse-making on a tennis court. By this point, we have heard every excuse under the sun, so this brings us to the most important question in tennis today: no, not how to beat Novak Djokovic, but rather, what is the perfect tennis excuse? It is a question that has been plaguing tennis' top scholars for decades now, and we at The Tennis Player's Excuse Handbook are here to solve tennis' greatest mystery once and for all.

As both a competitive junior and adult player myself, who has had their fair share of good but also very bad performances, I have had plenty of chances to develop the complex skill of tennis excuse-making. You see, what I have learned over the years is that tennis is different to all other sports. You are all alone out there, with so many factors that can affect your game, which not only makes it one of the hardest sports to play but also makes it one of the sports with the most reasons why things can go wrong. Were there bad conditions? Was your opponent, let's just say, being a bit 'eager' with their line calls? Did your racket let you down? All are valid excuses unique to every time you play, each giving us a different reason to blame our lousy performance on.

And that leads us to the most important lesson to take away from this book and for all you young tennis fans out there: It's never your fault. I'm sure that at some point in your life, you have found an excuse for playing badly, only for your coach or friend to turn around and tell you to take ownership of your poor performance. Well, we're here to flip the switch. We're here to show you perfectly curated excuses developed over centuries of bad performances that can take away your personal blame for any loss.

At the end of this book, you will no longer be saying things like, 'I lost that match because I didn't train hard enough', but rather, 'I would have won that match if it wasn't for that injury'.

And these are the most important lessons in tennis…. probably.

GAME, SET, EXCUSE

THE GREATEST EXCUSES IN PROFESSIONAL TENNIS HISTORY

'I was attacked by a baby kangaroo'
Caroline Wozniacki

We will start off with perhaps the greatest excuse in professional tennis history. Wozniacki appeared to have scratches on her legs before her victory over Anastasija Sevastova in the fourth round of the 2011 Australian Open, and to the amazement of all the reporters listening, said that it came from a baby kangaroo attack that had happened the night before while going for a walk in the park.

Sadly, to the disappointment of everyone who believed this wild story, she later came clean, admitting that she made the story up because what really happened was that she walked into a treadmill and was embarrassed by the slight injury.

THE EXCUSE METER

● ● ● ● ● ● ○ ○ ○

This would have been a slam-dunk 10/10 on the excuse meter, but she made one huge mistake: she went back on herself. You should learn two things from reading this book: one—it's never your fault, and two—always commit to your excuse, no matter how ridiculous or unbelievable it is.

You almost had them, Caroline.

'I kissed a girl'
Richard Gasquet

Some of you may remember the uproar when up-and-coming star Richard Gasquet tested positive for cocaine in March 2009, and that same group of you will probably also recall being in even more shock when his drug ban was overturned after his unlikely excuse proved plausible enough and he was excused of any wrongdoing. Gasquet claimed that the illegal drug was only in his system because he had kissed a girl in a nightclub who had taken the substance, and to the shock of everyone, the ITF panel believed this. To this day, it still goes down as perhaps the most unlikely doping ban that was overturned in tennis, and Gasquet should count himself very fortunate.

THE EXCUSE METER

● ● ● ● ● ● ● ● ○

Obviously, I wouldn't recommend this one to anyone, but the sheer boldness to get away with it means it has to be high up on the excuse scale.

'The court smelled like onions'
Andy Murray

After a 2017 Davis Cup match, Andy Murray came out with one of the funniest excuses of all time when he claimed he had been put off because the court "smells like onions". Apparently, the opponents had been eating lunch a little too close, and the odour had wafted onto the court, putting the Scot off.

THE EXCUSE METER

●●● ○○○○○○○

I respect the attempt, but come on, Andy. Who are you fooling? This excuse needs a few more layers if anyone is going to believe it really put you off (get it?). Maybe, if you want to really make this one work, pretend that the onions were making your eyes water, and it got so bad that you couldn't see the ball by the end of the match.

You see, Andy, the foundations were there; you just had to think it through a little further.

'It was in the steak'
Petr Korda

There have been many audacious excuses to get out of doping bans in tennis history, and Petr Korda's is right up there. The Czech player tested positive for the banned substance nandrolone in the 1990s, but rather than own up to voluntarily taking it, he blamed the positive test on the fact that he ate a lot of veal, which has small traces of nandrolone inside it. Seems plausible, right? That's what we tennis fans thought as well until scientists revealed that Korda would have to have eaten 40 calves per day for 20 years to get his levels that high. It turns out that Petr didn't think that one through too well after all.

THE EXCUSE METER

This had the makings of a top-tier excuse, but you forgot about one thing, Petr: the scientists. Remember, folks, you always need to back your excuses up with hard scientific facts that can withstand even the highest scrutiny. I hope you learned your lesson, Petr.

5

'Too much chocolate' Serena Williams

It isn't often that Serena Williams, perhaps the greatest player of all time, seems relatable to us mere mortals, but her excuse after a poor performance at the 2016 Australian Open is probably far too familiar for all of us reading. She said she had eaten too many sweets and chocolates the night before and joked that this was the reason that she felt sluggish on court. Now, I am of the strong opinion that there is no such thing as too much chocolate, but I guess when you have a Grand Slam match the day after, it might not be the wisest thing to do.

THE EXCUSE METER

● ● ● ● ● ● ○ ○ ○ ○

This is certainly a good one to keep in your back pocket if you are feeling a little slower than normal out there, but I think there are more effective excuses in the book. Try to steer clear of excuses that put yourself at the centre of the blame.

Remember, it's never your fault. Next time, Serena, try blaming the opponent.

'I'm pregnant'
Sesil Karatancheva

This next excuse is perhaps the most audacious in the whole book, and despite the poor execution, you have to admire the boldness. Bulgarian player Karatancheva blamed one of her nandrolone positive tests on the fact that she was pregnant. Seems possible, right? Well, I've missed one key detail - she wasn't actually pregnant, and this showed in the urine samples.

THE EXCUSE METER

Come on, Sesil, blaming the positive test on pregnancy is already a stretch, but doing so when you're not even pregnant is just crazy.

If you do ever find yourself pregnant, then this is an absolute gold mine of excuses, not for taking illegal drugs, of course, but for pretty much anything else.

For those nine months, nothing that you do is your fault, and you must make sure that you take advantage of every pregnancy-related excuse possible!

'_I saw Roger Federer watching me_'
Fabio Fognini

Now, I know that if Roger Federer was watching me play tennis, I'd probably forget to breathe, let alone be able to swing a racket. So, I think we can all understand where Fabio was coming from here. This probably explains why the flamboyant Italian was never able to win a set against the Swiss legend in their four encounters.

THE EXCUSE METER
● ● ● ● ● ● ● ● ○ ○

If any of you reading this ever get the opportunity to play in front of Federer, then it will be a slam-dunk 10/10 excuse. Who could ever expect you to perform there? However, Fabio was already a seasoned pro by 2014 when he gave this excuse, so we've had to drop this excuse down to a respectable eight on the excuse meter.

'I was stung by a bee'
Tommy Haas

At least once a year, players will have a problem with a bee attack on court. Just look at when Carlos Alcaraz had to run away from a literal swarm of bees at Indian Wells in 2024, but luckily for Carlitos, he avoided being stung. The same can't be said for Tommy Haas at the 2007 US Open, who was stung during a disappointing straight-sets defeat to Nikolay Davydenko. Fortunately, the German was able to take away any blame from his own game and blame it all on that dastardly stinging machine.

THE EXCUSE METER

● ● ● ● ● ● ● ○ ○ ○

This is an excellent excuse you should always have in the locker after a particularly bad day. The best thing is that bees are so small that there is no way your opponent could ever see if there really was a bee attacking you. You can simply start swatting at the air with your racket until the fake swarm of bees has gone away. Not after one has 'stung' you on your playing arm, of course.

'When he serves, he farts'
Lighton Ndefwayl

Get ready for the funniest, most ridiculous and almost certainly bitterest excuse in the history of tennis. It is an excuse that is so hilariously crazy that it needs no further explanation. So, sit back, relax and get ready to hear a direct quote from Lighton Ndefwayl after one of his losses in 1992.

"Bwayla is a stupid man and a hopeless player. He has a huge nose and is cross-eyed. Girls hate him. He beat me because my jockstrap was too tight and because when he serves, he farts, and that made me lose my concentration, for which I am famous throughout Zambia."

THE EXCUSE METER
● ● ● ● ● ● ● ● ● ●

Wow, where do we begin with this one? You may have noticed that this is our first and only 10/10 score on the excuse meter, but come on, this is the stuff of legends.

Lighton Ndefwayl, you may not be remembered in the history books for your tennis ability, but you certainly are the Novak Djokovic of tennis excuses.

⑩

'My girlfriend left me'
Goran Ivanišević

Oh, Goran. I'm sure too many of us can sympathise with you on this one. The big-serving Croat once blamed a bad defeat on his girlfriend breaking up with him, saying he was too emotional to focus.

We can't feel too sorry for him, though. Not long after, he became the first and only men's player to win a Grand Slam as a wildcard.

THE EXCUSE METER

● ● ● ● ● ● ● ○ ○

While this is one of the sadder excuses, it is also one of the most effective. Not even the harshest of critics can delve deeper into why you played badly after pulling this one out.

Did your partner leave you one year ago? No problem! There's your excuse. Not only is it incredibly effective, but it can also be one of the most long-lasting excuses in the book.

'A butterfly flew into my eye'
Novak Djokovic

Djokovic has had his fair share of good excuses over the years, but this one perhaps wasn't his most convincing. Djokovic claimed to have lost his concentration during a game at the 2008 Australian Open after a butterfly flew into his eye. Now, you get some sympathy when it's a swarm of bees with stingers on the attack, but when it's just a butterfly, I think you can handle it, Novak.

Anyway, it can't have put him off too much because a few days later, he was lifting his first Grand Slam trophy after beating Jo-Wilfried Tsonga in the final.

THE EXCUSE METER

If we're going to pick an animal 'attack' as an excuse, it can't be something where everyone's first thought is going to be "oh, how cute". While I can imagine that it did put the Serb off for a brief moment, he would have needed a much stronger excuse had he actually gone on to lose the match.

12

'It was my fitness trainer'
Jannik Sinner

Here comes one that has been dividing tennis fans worldwide recently and one that I am sure you are all aware of. Sinner twice tested positive for the anabolic steroid clostebol in March 2024 but was able to explain it away by saying that his physio had massaged a spray containing the substance into him while giving him treatment after a training session.

The tennis world seems to agree that it entered Sinner's body accidentally and was such a low amount that I can't have helped his performances, but for many, this is irrelevant. It has become a touchy subject amongst tennis fans, with many comparing it to similar cases in the past where players were banned, saying that Sinner has received special treatment.

THE EXCUSE METER

● ● ● ● ● ● ● ○ ○

Whether you sympathise with him or not, very few can deny that Sinner has found a very valid and believable excuse that thoroughly deserves its 7/10 on the excuse meter. That being said, those who believe he should be banned may have the last laugh, with the news recently coming out that WADA has appealed the previous ruling of no negligence.

Either way, it's certainly one of the most famous excuses.

'I drank too much pickle juice'
Jack Sock

In 2017, Jack Sock produced one of the funnier reasons why he played a poor match: because he had drunk 700ml of pickle juice before the match, making him feel "horrible". It may sound incredibly strange that a player would drink pickle juice before a match, but there is actually a reason why Jack was chugging down this sour concoction. Drinking pickle juice is a great way to replenish electrolytes and reduce the chances of cramping, so we can see what Jack was going for here, but apparently, there is a very distinct point where it stops being a help and starts becoming, well, horrible.

Maybe you should stick to pickleball Jack and stay off the juice.

THE EXCUSE METER

If you are looking for a strange but surprisingly scientific excuse, then the 'too much pickle juice' reason could be a good route to take. However, against 99% of casual players who aren't aware of the anti-cramping benefits that it gives you, it may just come off as a little strange.

'I blame my mothers pasta'
Sara Errani

As far as audacious excuses go to avoid a doping ban, Sara Errani's is right up there. She tested positive for the banned substance letrozole in 2017, and rather than own up to taking it herself, blamed it on her mother's pasta. It's not quite as ridiculous as it sounds, though, her mother was taking the drug to treat breast cancer at the time and claimed that she used the same surface to prepare the pasta that the letrozole had been resting on.

While it was recognised that there was only a 'light degree of fault' from Sara, it was not enough for her to avoid receiving a ten month ban.

THE EXCUSE METER

● ● ● ● ○ ○ ○ ○

Whether Sara intentionally took the substance or not, it certainly was a believable excuse. Unlike Petr Korda's wild theory, science appears to be on her side for this one, so despite not being successful, it deserves its 5/10 rating on the excuse scale.

⑮

'I was thinking about a swimming pool'
Marat Safin

We move from one of the more serious excuses in the book to one of the most light-hearted ones. Flashy player Marat Safin once blamed losing his concentration on a big point in a match because he was thinking about being in a swimming pool rather than a tennis court. I think we all dream about being in a nice swimming pool somewhere hot, Marat, but not at a crucial point in a professional tennis match!

Either way, the excuse did little to earn him sympathy. Instead, it caused him to put even more blame on himself because it seemed like he didn't care.

....

THE EXCUSE METER

● ● ○ ○ ○ ○ ○ ○ ○ ○

....

Come on, Marat. You didn't think this one through, did you? There are literally hundreds of excuses you could have used, and the best you could think of is a swimming pool. We've said it before, but a good excuse always takes the blame away from you. Maybe if Marat had done some proper tennis reading (cough, cough, by reading this book), he could not only have taken all the blame away from his subpar performance but won the sympathy of anyone listening at the same time.

'I was attacked by birds'
Ernests Gulbis

When you hear someone say that birds attacked them, it sounds like quite a genuine excuse, right? Well, when Ernest Gulbis said this after a match at the 2014 French Open, he was perhaps exaggerating just a little. In reality, many birds were flying over the court, which had distracted the Latvian, but it was a long, long way off an 'attack'.

THE EXCUSE METER

An excuse like this could easily be a 6/10 for amateur players like you and me, but when you're a pro, and every match you play is recorded for the world to see, it becomes a little harder to exaggerate the truth. It certainly wasn't the first or the last time we saw the flamboyant Latvian lose his concentration during a match, so it's no surprise that he had to find some adventurous excuses along the way.

'Shouting is part of my game'
Michelle Larcher

So, unlike all the other excuses we've seen from the pros so far, this one isn't to explain a bad performance. Portuguese player Michelle Larcher de Brito was famous for being one of the louder grunters on Tour and was once told by a reporter that her "singing" was exasperating her opponents. Rather than back down and admit that it could be a little too much at times, she doubled down, saying that shouting is part of her game and "that's why she's successful".

THE EXCUSE METER

● ● ● ● ● ● ● ● ○ ○

While I think we can all respect this bold response, I think that I speak for everyone when I say that I am glad that not every player takes this approach to grunting. That being said, if you are ever approached by someone saying you are too loud on court, just follow in Michelle's footsteps. What can they say after that, anyway?

(18)

'I couldn't sleep because of the mosquitoes' David Ferrer

David Ferrer had the perfect response to a poor performance at the 2015 Australian Open - he had been kept awake by mosquitoes flying around his room all night and had barely slept. Unlike some of the other players we have seen in this list, David was always the epitome of professionalism, so this excuse was quickly accepted by the reporters listening, and suddenly, the blame had been completely shifted from him to something that was out of his control.

Master play David.

THE EXCUSE METER

● ● ● ● ● ● ○ ○ ○

Blaming a loss on a lousy sleep is always a top-tier excuse. No one can prove it, and there are so many reasons why you might have slept poorly. Did the neighbours keep you up all night because they were having a party, or did you get woken up in the middle of the night by a crying baby? They are all so effective and completely consequence-free.

If you really want to milk it, then why not add a bit of black eye shadow to make those bags under your eyes seem just that bit bigger? Then throw the odd yawn in there for good measure, just in case it wasn't obvious enough already.

I WASN'T READY

THE BEST PERSONAL EXCUSES

① I was being too nice with my line calls

"I gave them the benefit of the doubt on every call today. Then, when it was tight at the end, and I hit a shot that was close but looked in, what did they do? They called it out. Dammit, why didn't I do the same."

② I didn't have time to warm up

"These youngsters can step on court and get straight into a match. Not me. I need at least 20 minutes to get everything warmed up. That's why I lost the first set 6-0 today, and it had absolutely nothing to do with them being much better than I am."

③
I couldn't serve today because of my back

"My back was hurting so much today I couldn't serve at all at the end of the match. The pain strangely got worse the more I was losing, and then somehow made a full recovery straight after the match. What a mystery."

④
I didn't realise it was a full third set

"I'm feeling absolutely knackered going into this last set. I wonder if that's why they are insisting on playing a full third and not a match tiebreak."

⑤ I always start badly because I'm nervous

"I'm so tight at the start of every match, I might as well just start every match 2-0 down. How can people swing so freely to begin with? Oh well, at least it makes it exciting."

⑥ I never play well in the morning

"I always play so badly in the mornings. If the time says AM, then my mind is still half in bed where it belongs. I wonder if this has anything to do with why my opponent always asks me to play matches at 8 am."

7
I'm still coming back from an injury

"That week I took off because my ankle was sore five weeks ago is still costing me. If it weren't for that injury, I'd have won this match easily."

8
Basically every game went to deuce

"Yes, I lost 6-0 6-0, but it was actually really close. I was in it in every game and somehow got unlucky every time. If I can convert some of those deuce games next time, I'll definitely beat them."

9

I'd do just as well without any strings

"I framed so many balls today, I'd play just as well if I cut all my strings out."

10

I can't play match tiebreaks

"I always lose match tiebreaks. There's just something about them. I'd have won easily if we had played a full third set. Match tiebreaks are just a pure gamble."

⓫

I didn't have enough space behind the baseline

"I hit the back fence with my swing every time they hit a ball deep. What kind of courts are these?"

⓬

I haven't hit a ball for ages

"I haven't played tennis for two whole weeks. Yes, I've been playing tennis for 15 years, but how am I supposed to play my best after such a long break?"

13

It was so dark I could barely see the ball

"It was basically pitch black when we stopped playing. I could barely see my racket, let alone the ball. It must somehow have been darker for me than my opponent. Strange how that always happens."

14

I never play singles

"I'm just a doubles player. It's been years since I've played singles, and they're basically different sports."

15

I was distracted watching the pros on the court next to me

"How can I concentrate on my match when it's like the 2008 Nadal Federer Wimbledon final on the court next to me?"

16

They didn't want to change ends

"It's funny, every time the sun was in their eyes, they always asked to change ends. But when the sun was in my eyes, they were always perfectly happy staying where they were."

17

My doubles partner let me down

"I played great today, but my partner... oh boy. Not even Martina Navratilova could have won playing with them today."

18

My tennis elbow was flaring up

"I could barely hold the racket at the end of the match, my tennis elbow was so bad. And yes, it's just a strange coincidence that I only get tennis elbow when I'm losing. Isn't it the same for everyone?"

19

It was way too cold to play

"I could barely grip my racket today, my hands were so cold. What do they expect me to do, play with woolly gloves on?"

20

I don't care about the results now, I'm playing for the future

"Yes, I went for 84 winners today and missed nearly all of them. But that doesn't matter. I may be losing now, but just you wait until the future when I'm playing like the pros."

(21) I got nervous

"I'd be world number one if I didn't get nervous in matches. I just freeze up when it gets tight."

(22) I hate playing short sets

"Who thought of changing sets from six games to four? I have time to recover from a bad start in a normal set, but with short sets, the match is basically over before it has begun."

㉓ The side fence was too close

"It was so unfair. Every time they hit a slice serve, the ball was in the side fence before I could hit it. Yes, it was the same for me. But that's not the point."

㉔ I couldn't move properly because of my knee

"I would have won that match easily if my knee wasn't playing up. All they started doing was moving me from side to side. I would never have done that to an injured player."

(25) I couldn't get a rhythm

"I hate playing against players like that. I feel like I'm so much better than they are, but they play such a strange style that I can never get a rhythm."

(26) I'm too old to run for all these drop shots

"These kids think it's fun to keep hitting drop shots against me. Just wait until you're my age, and we'll see who's the better player."

㉗
It was our first time playing together

"We need time to gel together as a pair. We'll beat them next time we play, for sure."

㉘
I broke a string

"I was completely dominating until I broke a string. It changed the whole match around."

29
I lost all of the sudden death deuces

"The whole point of deuce is you need to win two points to win the game. Who decided to make tennis quicker and change it to just one? And how could I lose every single one in the match?"

30
The court next to me was being too loud

"I could barely hear myself think, let alone play tennis."

31

I can't play on fast courts

"The serves were coming through so fast, I hit every return late."

32

My hands were too sweaty

"Every time I hit a serve, I thought my racket would fly out of my hand. There's no way I would have been broken all match if I could have gone for it properly."

(33)

They hit every shot to my backhand

"I feel like I only hit about three forehands all match. I understand playing to the opponent's weakness, but that was too much."

IT'S NOT MY FAULT

MARVELLOUS OPPONENT-BASED EXCUSES

① I can't play against lefties

"The ball was spinning the wrong way every time. There's just something so weird about returning a left-handed serve."

② Their line calls were horrendous!

"They were so generous at the start of the set when it didn't count, but as soon as it got tight, their eyes apparently started playing tricks on them. You know the lines are in, right?"

③ The net was rigged against me

"They got a net cord on set point; what could I do? The universe was clearly against me today."

④ I can't play against pushers

"I was playing nice, proper tennis, and all they did was push the ball around. I'd rather lose than play like that."

⑤

They only beat me because it was their home club

"They just knew the courts so much better than I did. I'd get them if it were anywhere else."

⑥

It all changed after they took a toilet break

"I bet they didn't even need the toilet. They only did it to break my rhythm and change the momentum. And what's even worse is that it worked!"

7

They were grunting too loud

"How could I concentrate on my game when all I could hear was them screaming on the other side? It's okay when it's Sharapova vs Serena in a Grand Slam final, but when Margaret does it at 8 am on a Sunday down at the local club, it's a bit much."

8

They were hitting underarm serves

"It's just such bad sportsmanship. If they want to win that way, then fine. I stopped running for them out of protest."

⑨ They wouldn't stop, even though it was raining and getting dangerous

"They wanted to stop earlier when I was winning and it started drizzling, but as soon as they took the lead, then surprise, surprise, they wouldn't stop no matter how much it rained."

⑩ They won all the big points

"I had way more break points than they did. If only I'd have been able to convert them like they did, I would have won that match."

11

All they were is a big serve

"All they are is serve, serve, serve. Any time I made the return, they were nothing special. Let's play without serves and see who wins then."

12

They were moon-balling

"Their balls were going so high in the air, they practically had snow on them by the time they came down."

13

They called a ball out on clay and showed the wrong mark

"That's a mark from a serve I hit 10 minutes ago. How can they even pretend that's the proper mark?"

14

They were getting too pumped up

"When a player starts fist-pumping in your friendly doubles game on a Sunday morning, sometimes it's best to just let them win."

15

They ran around every backhand

"Tennis is a game of both forehands and backhands, but clearly, they've not quite understood this. Every time I found their backhand, I won the point, but they just always ran around it."

16

They were so tactical with their let calls

"When they had a smash on top of the net and a ball rolled onto the court, what did I do? Let them finish the point. But as soon as I had an easy ball and the same happened, they called a let! That's just bad etiquette."

17

They questioned every one of my calls

Ball flies two metres out... "Are you sure that was long? I think it might have caught the back of the line. Shall we play two?"

18

They were slapping every ball

"All they did was slap the ball, and somehow it went in every time. There's no way they could do that again."

19

They were standing extra close on their returns to put me off

"They stood inside the line when I was bouncing the ball, and then when I served, they were miraculously behind the baseline again."

20

It was their first match of the day

"I'm knackered from my match this morning while they've come in completely fresh. The pros don't play two matches in a day, so why should we?"

21

They took it way too seriously

"I was just there for a bit of fun, but they were acting like it was the final of Wimbledon."

22

All they did was come to the net

"Every time I looked up, they had rushed to the net. We had them from the back of the court every time, but as soon as they came forward, they turned into the Bryan brothers."

(23)

They were foot faulting on every serve

"I don't take tennis too seriously, but come on. This is just unfair. They were stood inside the baseline every time when they were hitting their serve. They can basically reach over the net from there."

(24)

They hit with way too much topspin

"Every ball I hit was bouncing over my head. I was hitting my shots from so far behind the baseline that I could barely hit it over the net. How am I supposed to play against that?"

(25) They had all the latest gear

"How can I beat them if I'm playing with a 20-year-old racket and they have the brand new Babolat Pure Aero 98? Turns out they had all the gear and some idea."

(26) They were a rule book warrior

"I was sat down at the change of ends, and suddenly they had a stopwatch out saying I had 10 seconds out of my 90 left over. Who does that?"

㉗

They had a delayed grunt

"Grunting is annoying, but I can deal with it. What I can't deal with is someone starting their grunt while I'm hitting my shot."

㉘

They hit the ball too flat

"Their shots came through so low and fast. Haven't they heard of a western grip?"

㉙

They're more used to this surface than I am

"How are they moving so much better than me? The only logical answer is that they play on this surface way more than I do. Nothing to do with them just being a better mover than me."

㉚

They said they weren't ready when I hit my serve

"They were so ready for that. What a coincidence that they weren't ready just when I hit my best serve of the match."

㉛ They were a junk-baller

"I couldn't get any rhythm today. Every shot was something different: short slice, moon ball, drop shot, you name it. How could I play against that?"

㉜ They said come on after I hit a double fault

"It's fine if they hit a good shot, but really, after I've just hit a double fault. Come on. Oh wait, now I've said it as well."

③③ Their net player in doubles was trying to put me off

"Are you really going to stand closer to the service box I'm serving into just to put me off?"

③④ They went for the towel after every point

"Not even the pros go to the towel after every point, and it wasn't even hot today! It slowed the match down so much."

35

They kept messing their ball toss up

"Once or twice is fine. Not every time you serve. I never knew when they were actually going to hit it."

36

They called it out because they saw the mark... but it's a hard court?!

"I have no issue with calling a ball out because you can see the mark... if it's a clay court! How can you possibly see a mark on a hard court?"

37

They didn't have any pockets in their shorts

"Every time they missed a first serve, they had to go to the back of the court and get a new ball. Who buys shorts without pockets anyway?"

38

It was like playing against a brick wall

"Seriously, do they ever miss? How can anyone ever beat someone like that? I might as well play against my house next time."

39

All they did was slice it

"I appreciate a good slice, but seriously, every shot? My back was hurting at the end because I had to get so low to every shot."

40

They were rushing me

"Seriously? They must have been taking five seconds between each point. I don't like it when players take too long between points, just like anyone else, but I need at least some time to regroup."

BLAME
THE ELEMENTS

EXCUSES ABOUT THE CONDITIONS

① The sun was in my eyes

"Every time I threw the ball up to serve, I was not only blinded by the sun, but the sun also swallowed the ball up. I'd have had as much luck if I just shut my eyes."

② The court was too slippery

"It was way too wet to move on that court. I've never slid so much in my life, and it was a hard court."

3

I kept getting bad bounces

"I've never seen someone hit as many lines or patches of clay in my life. The ball was bouncing left, right, and well, not centre."

4

I lost the ball in their ball toss

"Really? Whose idea was it to paint the wall white behind the court."

⑤

It was so windy it completely put me off my ball toss

"Serving isn't the easiest on the best of days, but when my toss is being blown anywhere but over my head, it's virtually impossible."

⑥

The sun only came out when I was serving

"Somehow, defying all logic, the sun went away every time my opponent went to serve. Even the elements were against me today."

I can't play on anything apart from acrylic anymore

"I used to play on asphalt and concrete all the time, but after switching to acrylic, I can't go back."

The wind picked up every time I served

"Every time they served, there was just a light breeze, but every time I stepped up to the baseline, out came the hurricane-force winds. Not even John Isner could have coped with that today."

Those clay courts hadn't been swept for days

"There were mountains of clay at the side of the court, but the baseline looked like an orange hard court. There's no way I could trust myself to slide out there today."

NEW BALLS PLEASE

EVERYDAY EQUIPMENT EXCUSES IN TENNIS

① My strings were too loose

"My strings were like a trampoline today, every ball was flying long. It definitely has nothing to do with me going bigger on my shots. No, can only be the strings."

② I lost my shock absorber

"As soon as I lost my dampener, I couldn't play. Somehow, it completely changed how the racket felt, and I didn't want to get tennis elbow. That's the only reason I lost the second set 6-0, clearly."

③ The balls were too old

"I'm not saying we need brand new balls every time, but the balls today would have been more suitable for my dog, not our match."

④ I forgot my cap

"I couldn't see a thing without my cap today, and when I suggested we move indoors, my opponent said no!"

5

I couldn't see the lines

"The baseline was covered in clay all match, and I couldn't see it at all. Yes, I've been playing for ten years, but somehow, I completely forgot how big a tennis court was today."

6

My strings broke mid-match

"I was playing so well until my strings broke. Then, even though my spare racket was the exact same, the match changed completely. I guess those were my lucky strings."

7

My racket was too light

"I couldn't get any power today, it felt like I was playing with a children's racket. It definitely needs to be heavier."

8

We didn't have any singles sticks

"I can't believe that winner they hit on match point. That would so have gone in the net if we had singles sticks."

9

I'm not used to playing with new balls

"Every time we train, it's with old balls. So when I step into a match with new balls, it feels like a completely different sport. I feel like I just tap the ball, but somehow, it flies five metres long every time."

10

My grip was too old

"I haven't changed that grip all year. Every time I hit a forehand, I thought it was going to come flying out of my hand."

⑪
I still had the factory strings in

"Everyone else always complains about the factory strings in a new racket, but I never got it... until today. Get me some scissors to cut these out pronto."

⑫
The balls fluffed up too much

"The court completely chewed the balls up today, they had practically doubled in size by the end of the match. Now I know why the pros change balls every nine games."

13

I had to borrow a racket

"As soon as I play with anyone else's racket, you can forget it. Any chance of me playing well today was gone as soon as I forgot mine."

14

The net was too high

"I hit so many serves in the net today, it was definitely too high. There's no way it was anything to do with my serve. Nope, has to be the net."

15
I had a hole in my shoe

"That completely stopped me from moving properly today. I felt like I would not just have a hole in my shoe at the end of the match, but my foot as well."

16
The balls got too wet

"There's nothing like getting splashed in the face every time you hit the ball."

17

My strings were too old

"I can't believe those strings are still hanging on. I only lost that match because I was trying to hit the ball harder to finally break them."

18

I can't play with those balls

"Really, who can play properly with those balls? The only balls worth playing with are Head ATP and Wilson USO."

YOU CANNOT BE SERIOUS

TIMELESS TENNIS COMPLAINTS

①

Players taking your court who haven't booked

Every club member will experience this on a regular basis. You turn up to play at your regular club session that you book every week, only for two people to be playing on your court who haven't booked. If you're feeling really friendly, you might play on another court and run the risk of someone else who has booked kicking you off, or you apologetically chuck the two players off while they pretend not to know that you need to book a court to play.

②

When players always forget to bring balls

Forgetting to bring balls every now and then is not a problem at all, but when it's every time, it's just annoying. And balls aren't cheap!

3

People walking behind your court when you're playing a point

This is a tennis complaint as old as time. You'll be having the best rally of the match, and just as you're about to finish the point with a sublime winner, a person will aimlessly walk across the back of the court, putting you off from the rally of the century. What can make this one even more painful is when your opponent calls a let, and you mess up the replayed point with a double fault.

4

Playing with an odd number

We've all been there. You've put a message in the tennis group chat and have a game of singles or doubles lined up. And then, at the very last minute, someone else chimes up and decides to ruin the numbers and make it a three or a five.

⑤
People cancelling if there is a 5% chance of rain

Picture this: you've been looking forward to playing tennis all week, and then the night before match day, you get a message from your opponent saying, "There's a small chance of rain tomorrow. Shall we postpone until next week?" The worst!

⑥
Players not clearing balls off the court before the point starts

This one might not affect you personally, but nothing puts me more on edge than when players leave balls lying around all over the court, just waiting for them to step on and twist their ankle. The all time most uncomfortable is the player who doesn't have any pockets and instead puts the second ball on the baseline next to them.

Players withdrawing just before a match is finished

At least with this one, you still get the win, so it isn't the worst thing in the world. But have you ever had a player retire just before you are about to win the match? Like, come on. If you're 6-1 5-0 down, unless you're on death's door, have the dignity to finish the last game rather than retire.

When players exclusively play singles or doubles

Some players prefer singles, while others are better at doubles, but then there are those players who outright refuse to play anything that isn't their speciality. Having a preference is fine, but refusing to play one can be inconvenient. Besides, they're both part of the sport, right?

⑨ Who's got money for the flood lights?

This can be annoying in two different ways: either no one has the change needed for the floodlights, and you have to stop playing early, or everyone else conveniently forgets their petty cash every week, and you're the one paying to keep the match going.

⑩ Players not sweeping the clay court after they are finished

If you're not used to playing on clay courts, then this might not seem like such a big deal, but for those of you who regularly play on the dirt, this is perhaps the most common complaint. Nothing is worse than having to spend the first five minutes of your hour-long session sweeping the court after the players before you 'forgot'.

Hitting your best serve of the match, only for it to skim the top of the net

We've all experienced this. You smash down your best serve of the match - maybe it's even an ace - only for it to skim the top of the net and be a let. And, of course, the next one always ends up missing.

COURTSIDE CLICHÉS

CLASSIC TENNIS STEREOTYPES

1

Bag bigger than they are

This is a personal favourite of mine. If you've ever played a junior tournament or have taken your kids to one, you'll know exactly what I mean. This will be a junior who is barely tall enough to look over the net and yet has a 15-racket bag bigger than they are. They are often so big that the bag even drags behind them on the floor. Ironically, as tennis players get older and taller, their bags do the opposite and get smaller until they become adults and start leaving their bags at home and only bring a racket and a water bottle.

2

What's the score again?

We all know this type of player. It could be their set point at 6-5 in the tiebreak, and you would hear them say, "What's the score again?" Sometimes, it can be a fun game to make up an entirely different score just to see what you can get away with.

3

The grunt machine

Despite being completely harmless, this type of player will likely grind your gears more than any other. It doesn't matter where they are playing, whether it's at a tournament on the weekend or just warming up in a friendly game of doubles; you will be able to hear them from miles away. Rumour has it they even grunt when they open the door to the clubhouse.

4

All the gear, no idea

We've all come across this player. They have three brand new rackets, sweatbands and a huge bag, only to step on court and not be able to hit a ball. Meanwhile, you've probably turned up with one racket, no water bottle and some running shoes, yet beat them 6-0 6-0.

⑤ Mr unconventional

This is about that one player at your local club who has the craziest, most unorthodox technique but somehow, defying all laws of physics, manages to make it work. You will likely watch them with a strange mixture of admiration and bewilderment, all the time wondering if they have ever had a coaching session.

⑥ The self-talker

This is a special kind of player who can have a full-blown conversation with themselves if things aren't going their way. There will be gasps of joy, stern words about what they're doing wrong, and if you're lucky, they may even refer to themselves in the third person.

⑦ Serial sweater

This player once again defies the laws of physics, with some referring to it as the Andy Roddick syndrome. No matter what temperature it is, they will turn up with a fresh shirt, and somehow, after just one game, that shirt will have completely changed colour with sweat, and when you change ends, you'll find that the baseline is drenched in water.

⑧ The tortoise

It doesn't matter how fit and agile this player is; as soon as the point is over, something happens to them, and they start moving in slow motion. Maybe their parents were sloths. Who knows? Doctors are yet to find the reason for this tennis condition.

⑨ Anger management

Many players get frustrated on court, but each club has that one player who always takes it too far, and you genuinely think has anger issues. Off the court, they are usually the nicest person ever, but as soon as the first point is played - children beware - with this player, there will likely be rackets flying and curse words aplenty.

⑩ The secret full-time player

You may think this is a player who just plays with you once a week, but when you ask around at the local club, you will find that six other players also play with them once a week, and they are training as much as Iga Świątek.

11

The bandit

The lowly ranked player who turns up to a tournament and surprises everyone by beating players they never should have had a chance against on paper. A bandit is usually a once-great player who has been out with injury for a while or a great player who doesn't play many tournaments.

12

The cheater

Unfortunately, this one is all too common. They're usually a very fair line caller at the start of the match, but as soon as it's a big point and the ball goes near the line, you'd best believe they will confidently stick out their finger and yell "out".

⑬ Terrible ball toss

This player somehow defies all logic by throwing the ball anywhere but over their head. After two or three tries of the ball veering dangerously away from them, they will often get frustrated and hit their serve, no matter how bad the toss was, resulting in some hilarious outcomes.

⑭ Plays for the outfits

This player plays tennis for one thing and one thing only: the outfits. They don't care what the result is; the only real winner is the player with the most style.

15

The tireless competitor

You could play a five-hour match against this sort of player, and at the end, they'll be almost sure to say, "Just one more set?". They have an engine that could rival Mo Farah and would play tennis all day, every day, if given the chance.

Printed in Dunstable, United Kingdom